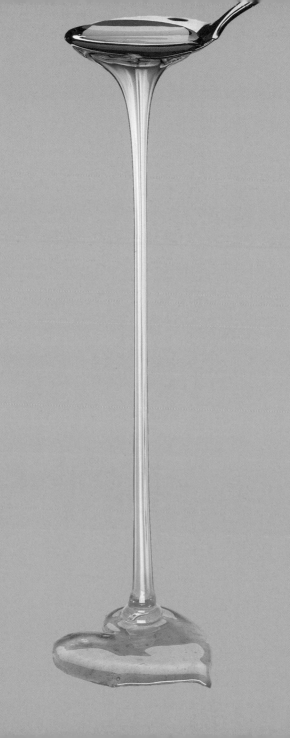

THE
LYLE'S GOLDEN SYRUP
COOKBOOK

PAUL HARTLEY

ABSOLUTE PRESS

First published in Great Britain in 2008
by **Absolute Press**
Scarborough House
29 James Street West
Bath BA1 2BT

Phone 44 (0) 1225 316013
Fax 44 (0) 1225 445836
E-mail info@absolutepress.co.uk
Website www.absolutepress.co.uk

© Absolute Press, 2008
Text copyright © Paul Hartley, 2008

Publisher Jon Croft
Commissioning Editor Meg Avent
Designer Matt Inwood
Publishing Assistant Andrea O' Connor
Photography Andy Davis
Props Stylist Cynthia Inions
Food Stylist Tina Boughey

In association with www.breakfastandbrunch.com.

A catalogue record of this book is available from the
British Library

ISBN 9781904573791

Printed and bound by 1010 Printing International, China

The Lyle's trademarks and copyrighted materials used in
this book are owned exclusively by Tate & Lyle PLC and
are used with permission.

CONTENTS

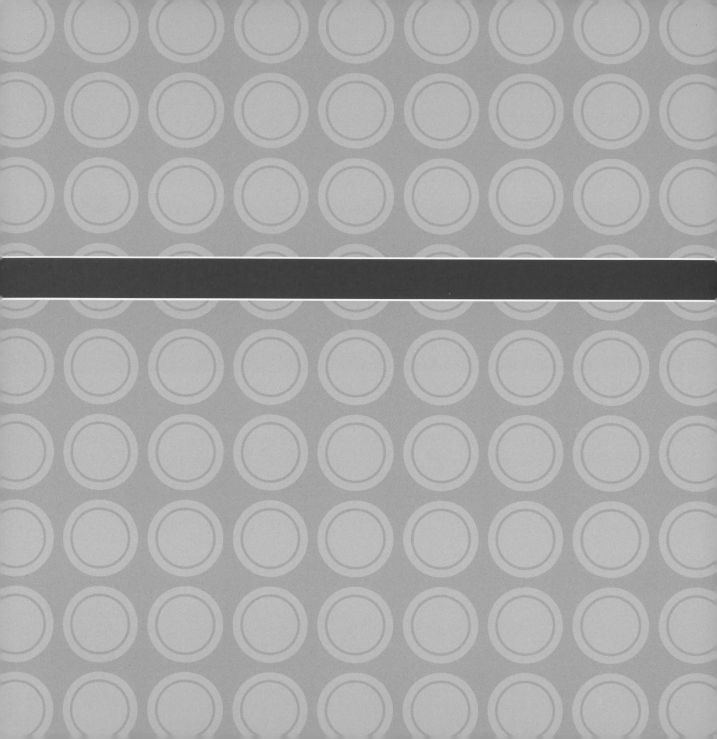

THE
LYLE'S GOLDEN SYRUP

BAKED APPLES WITH PRUNES IN CINNAMON SYRUP

Just a fantastic classic example of baked apples packed with delicious, spicy flavours. This dish has a wow factor in colour, texture and taste.

SERVES 4

100g semi-dried prunes, stoned
2 tablespoons Armagnac (or brandy)
$\frac{1}{2}$ teaspoon ground cinnamon
40g pecan nuts, finely chopped
50g dark muscovado sugar
4 tablespoons Lyle's Golden Syrup, plus extra for coating
4 apples, approx. 175g each (Cox's or Golden Delicious are good)

Preheat the oven to 150F/300C/Gas 2.

Chop up the prunes and put them into a bowl with the Armagnac, cinnamon, nuts, sugar and golden syrup and leave aside to infuse.

Wash, dry and core the apples but do not peel. The easy way to core the apples is using a long thin knife or a potato peeler to make a circular hole about 3cm diameter right through the centre of the apple. Chop up the flesh, rejecting the pips and core you have just removed, and add it to the prune stuffing mixture.

Coat the apples with golden syrup by pouring the syrup and twirling the apples as you go. Then sit them in a greased ovenproof baking dish making sure they don't touch. Pack each one with the syrupy prune stuffing – don't worry about any overflow as it all adds to the rustic charm of the dish. Drizzle with any of the remaining juices.

Bake in the oven for 40–45 minutes, basting once or twice while they cook. Allow to cool a little before serving with good hot thick creamy custard. These are particularly good sitting on Cinnamon Gingerbread Hearts (see page 40).

SKY-HIGH LYLE'S

IF YOU WERE TO STACK EVERY TIN OF LYLE'S GOLDEN SYRUP SOLD IN EUROPE ALONE EACH YEAR, THE COLUMN WOULD STRETCH TO MORE THAN 1,500 TIMES THE HEIGHT OF THE WORLD'S TALLEST BUILDING.

SALMON KEBABS WITH LIME & SYRUP

Gorgeous chunks of pink fish infused with sharp lime and sweet syrup.

SERVES 4

800g salmon fillet, skinned and cubed

For the marinade
zest of 1 lime and juice of 2 limes
1 stalk of fresh lemongrass, finely sliced
1 tablespoon light soy sauce
1 tablespoon fish sauce
2 tablespoons Lyle's Golden Syrup

4 sheets of medium egg noodles
chopped chives to garnish

Put the cubes of salmon fillet into a large, shallow dish. In a bowl mix together the ingredients for the marinade until well blended and then pour over the salmon.

Cover with clingfilm and leave in the fridge for at least 2 hours, turning the fish once during this time. Soak some wooden skewers in water to prevent them burning later.

Bring a pan of water to the boil. Add the noodles and then remove from the heat and cover with a lid. After a couple of minutes swizzle the noodles about with a fork to loosen them then cover again and leave for 5 minutes. Drain, return them to the pan and add a couple of tablespoons of the marinade to the noodles. Keep them warm while you finish the salmon.

Line a grill pan with foil and lightly oil the grill rack. Thread the salmon cubes onto the skewers and grill under a medium heat for 3–4 minutes on each side basting with some of the marinade. Serve the kebabs on top of the noodles scattered with chopped chives.

LYLE'S LEGEND & LORE
TREACLE MINES

TREACLE MINES have been a standing British joke for many, many years. It's a story that has been passed down from one generation to the next, just like the exotic myth of the Spaghetti Tree. What helps to make the story plausible to children is that treacle is darker than syrup and its extraction in this darkened raw state seems to bear some resemblance to the mining for coal. As for the science behind this sticky underground story, well, explanations range from claims that the treacle got there when Cromwell's army buried leaking barrels of molasses, to the fib of fossilised prehistoric sugar cane beds!

OATY MIXED BERRY CRUMBLE

These are great fun to cook with the kids and I promise they will love it as long as you don't tell them it's full of oaty goodness.

SERVES 4

450g mixed berries (such as blackcurrants, redcurrants, blueberries, raspberries)
2 tablespoons Lyle's Golden Syrup
75g butter (from the fridge)
100g plain flour
50g Demerara sugar
50g porridge oats
25g flaked almonds or mixed nuts (well crushed)
pinch ground cinnamon

Preheat the oven to 200C/400F/Gas 6. Lightly grease the inside of a 23cm/9" round ovenproof dish.

If you are using berries from the freezer they can be used from frozen. Simply put them in the dish and drizzle with the golden syrup, they will release their own juice. If you are using fresh berries in season it is worth adding a couple of tablespoons of fruit juice as well as the syrup. Spread the berries in the dish and press down gently and evenly.

Cut the butter into small cubes and put in a large bowl with the flour. Gently rub the two together with your fingertips. When you arrive at a texture like breadcrumbs add the sugar, oats, almonds and cinnamon and blend in well.

Spread the crumble mix loosely over the berries – a little higher in the centre as it may sink a little when cooking. You can sprinkle a little more sugar on top for extra crunch if you wish. Bake in the oven for 30–35 minutes, until golden brown. Great served with dollops of fruit sorbet.

'HOME SWEET HOME'
FROM THE PAINTING BY G.E. COLLINS R.B.A., 1905

GLAZED SAUSAGE TOAD IN THE HOLE

SERVES 4–6

150g plain flour
Salt and freshly milled black pepper
2 medium free-range eggs
150ml semi-skimmed milk mixed with 150ml cold water
6 free-range pork sausages
2 tablespoons Lyle's Golden Syrup
2 tablespoons lard

Preheat the oven to 220C/425F/Gas 7.

You will need a 23cm x 30cm (12" x 9") roasting tin.

Sieve the flour into a large bowl and season with salt and pepper. Make a well in the centre and crack in the eggs. Using an electric whisk slowly mix the flour with the eggs then gradually add the milk and water. Whisk until you have a smooth batter and then leave aside until ready to use.

Line a grill pan with foil, put the sausages on the rack and brush generously with the golden syrup. Grill them very gently, basting frequently with the syrup until they are golden and cooked through.

Heat the lard in a roasting tin in the top of the oven for 5 minutes until its shimmering hot. Lard has a higher smoking point than vegetable oil, which is crucial for good Yorkshire pudding – puffy and crispy. The hotter the fat is when the batter first hits it the better the end result. Take the tin out of the oven and put it over a medium heat on top of the cooker while you quickly and carefully (taking care of any spitting fat) arrange the sausages and immediately pour in the batter around the sausages. Put the tin straight into the top of the hot oven.

Bake for 30 minutes until the batter is puffed up, crispy edged and golden brown. Serve with good rich onion gravy and creamy mash.

TREACLE TART

Like all classic dishes there are many variations for making treacle tart. This is not a dish to get clever with – it's very easy to make and is indulgent with a capital 'I'.

SERVES 4–6

150g ready made shortcrust pastry
butter for greasing
150g fine fresh white breadcrumbs
zest of 1 lemon
454g tin of Lyle's Golden Syrup
lemon wedges to serve

You will need a lightly buttered 20cm/8" diameter flan dish.

Preheat the oven to 180C/350F/Gas 4.

Roll out the pastry fairly thin and line the flan dish. Make sure the pastry is gently pushed in around the edge to fully fit the dish and trim the excess pastry from the rim. Chill in the fridge for 15 minutes.

Mix together the breadcrumbs and the lemon zest and tip them into the flan, spreading them evenly over the base. Starting at the outside, in a circular motion working inwards, pour the contents of the golden syrup tin over the breadcrumbs – simple as that!

Put the treacle tart into the oven and cook for 10 minutes. Remove it from the oven and leave, as the treacle tart will continue cooking for a further 10 minutes all on its own.

Serve warm or cold with wedges of lemon and thick cream.

LYLE'S LEGEND & LORE

SCOTT'S SWEET TOOTH

IN 1912 a larder was set up in the frozen wastelands of Antarctica as part of the preparations for Captain Scott's epic journey to the South Pole. This store of food contained many provisions, including several large tins of Lyle's Golden Syrup. Tragically, Scott's expedition team died just ten miles short of the hut's salvation on their return from the Pole. Five months earlier, writing from his Cape Evans base, Scott wrote a letter to Lyle & Sons thanking them for the provisions of syrup: 'I have pleasure in informing you that your "Golden Syrup" has been in daily use in this Hut throughout the winter and has been much appreciated by Members of the Expedition. I regard it as a most desirable addition to necessary food articles of a Polar Expedition.'

BENGAL MANGO & GINGER CHUTNEY

Forget the Bengal tigers, this chutney will make your taste buds roar with delight.

MAKES 2 x 500ML JARS

6 medium fresh mangoes (about 2kg)
200g light muscovado sugar
200g Lyle's Golden Syrup
$\frac{1}{2}$ teaspoon cumin seeds
I teaspoon coriander seeds
$\frac{1}{2}$ teaspoon mustard seeds
8 cardamom pods
2 teaspoons paprika
$\frac{1}{2}$ teaspoon cayenne pepper
$\frac{1}{2}$ teaspoon turmeric
$\frac{1}{2}$ teaspoon ground cloves
50g root ginger, peeled and finely chopped
6 cloves garlic, peeled and finely chopped
I level teaspoon salt
500ml white vinegar (distilled malt)
2 medium onions, peeled and finely chopped

Peel and stone the mangoes over a large bowl to catch any juices and chop the flesh into cubes, scraping off any flesh clinging to the stone and skin. Add to this the sugar and syrup, mix well and leave to one side while you prepare the spices.

In a dry frying pan over a medium heat roast the cumin, coriander, mustard seeds and cardamom pods for a couple of minutes until they begin to crackle then tip them into a pestle and mortar and lightly crush to release the flavours.

Tip the roasted spices into a large heavy based pan and add the sweet mango mixture followed by all the remaining ingredients. Bring the mixture up to a simmer and then leave it very gently bubbling away for 3 hours. (Leave the lid on for the first hour and then uncovered for the rest.) Keep an eye after 2 hours as the liquid will almost evaporate and you will be left with a syrupy consistency which may tend to stick, so it will need to be stirred from time to time.

Remove the pan from the heat and leave to stand for at least 20 minutes before bottling in sterilised jars. Seal while still warm then leave to cool. Label and date your delicious chutney, which you will need to leave in a cool, dark place for 6 weeks to get the full and fantastic Indian flavour.

LEMON SYRUP PANCAKE STACK

This recipe was extracted from a New York street vendor, but improved by Lyle's Golden Syrup!

SERVES 4

For the pancakes
275g plain flour
2½ teaspoons baking powder
1 level teaspoon salt
3 tablespoons caster sugar
220ml milk
3 medium free-range eggs
50g unsalted butter, melted
250g Mascarpone
small punnet of blueberries

For the syrup
4 tablespoons Lyle's Golden Syrup
juice and zest of a large lemon

Sieve the flour, baking powder and salt into a bowl and add the caster sugar.

In another bowl whisk together the milk, eggs and melted butter. Add this to the flour mixture and gently whisk together to make a thick batter – it may not be totally smooth so don't worry as its best not to overwork the batter.

Lightly coat a large heavy based frying pan with a little oil and then drop in dessertspoons of the batter mixture in batches to fit the pan. Cook the pancakes over a low to medium heat until a few bubbles appear on the surface and the underside is golden, then flip them over. Keep going until you have used up all the batter, keeping the pancakes warm under foil.

In the meantime put the syrup and lemon in a pan and gently warm. On a warm serving plate arrange the pancakes in a stack spreading Mascarpone with whole blueberries between each pancake and finish by drizzling generously with the lemon syrup. Devour while still warm. Heavenly!

CASHEW, SOY & SYRUP-GLAZED GAMMON

This takes a little while to make but the end result is a delicious hot Sunday roast or, alternatively, try it sliced as a cold supper. There's a depth of flavour so good that its well worth the effort.

SERVES 6–8

1.5kg gammon or ham joint (choose one with a good area of fat and skin)
1 bay leaf
10 black peppercorns
1 onion, trimmed, unpeeled and chunked
1 tablespoon Demerara sugar
4 tablespoons Lyle's Golden Syrup
1 tablespoon dark soy sauce
2 tablespoons Lyle's Black Treacle
1 teaspoon Worcestershire sauce
100g unsalted cashew nuts, crushed

Place the gammon joint in a large pan, cover with cold water and add the bay, peppercorns, onion (the peel will really add to the flavour) and sugar and bring up to the boil. Reduce the heat down until just simmering and leave for 45 minutes. You may need to skim any residue off the surface of the water from time to time. Preheat the oven to 180C/350F/Gas 4.

Prepare a roasting tin with a piece of foil in it large enough to encase the joint. Carefully lift the gammon out of the pan, discarding the liquid and place it in the centre of the foil in the baking tin. Wrap the gammon to completely seal it with the foil and add boiling water to a depth of 2cm in the baking tray. Put it in the oven and roast for 45 minutes.

In a small bowl mix together the syrup, soy, molasses and Worcestershire sauce. Remove the gammon from the oven, allow to cool a little and then unwrap the foil, rolling it back down round the edge of the roasting pan and out of your way for the moment. Using a sharp knife, remove the skin and discard, leaving the fat in place. Make diagonal cuts both ways into the fat to create diamond shapes, being careful not to cut down into the meat – you will find the cuts will open up. Baste the fat well with the syrupy soy mixture into the open slits. Now bring back the foil and wrap it only over any parts that are lean meat so that all the criss-crossing is visible and sprinkle the chopped cashew nuts over all the basted fat. Return the joint to the oven for 10–15 minutes until it has a golden topping. Allow to cool for 15 minutes before serving hot, otherwise leave it to cool completely for the perfect supper.

COCONUT & CRANBERRY FLAPJACKS

A great combination of coconut and cranberry wrapped magnificently in a crunchy, oaty Jacket. Perfect for elevenses, a picnic, the kids' lunchbox or afternoon tea.

MAKES ABOUT 16 FLAPJACKS

200g unsalted butter
50g Demerara sugar
8 tablespoons Lyle's Golden Syrup
350g rolled oats
100g dessicated coconut
150g semi-dried cranberries

Preheat the oven to 150C/300F/Gas 2.

Heat the butter, sugar and syrup very gently in a saucepan until the butter has melted and all the sugar has dissolved. Remove from the heat and stir in the oats, coconut and cranberries.

Transfer the mixture to a suitable greased baking tray (20cm x 30cm /8"x12") and very gently press it in to fit the tin.

Bake in the centre of the oven for 40 minutes or until just golden. Allow to cool a little and cut into squares. The flapjacks can be stored in an airtight container for up to a week.

LYLE'S LOVES...
PANCAKES

LYLE'S GOLDEN SYRUP is the perfect topping for all kinds of sweet and savoury pancakes, but did you know...

Ralf Laue of Germany is the fastest pancake tosser in the world, flipping one pancake 416 times inside two minutes!

Since 1455, every Shrove Tuesday, the town of Olney, in England holds an annual pancake race. Legend has it that the tradition began when a woman of the town became so engrossed in making pancakes that she lost track of time until she heard the bells of the church ringing for the shriving service. Wearing her apron and still carrying her skillet with pancake, she set off for the church at a sprint. And so began the custom of the pancake race!

MULLED WINTER WINE

There really is nothing that will excite the senses more than mulled wine in winter, oozing warmth, flavour and aroma – all rolled up in one glass.

SERVES 6–8

1 medium orange
15 wholes cloves
300ml orange juice
75cl bottle red wine (Chilean Merlot is ideal)
4 tablespoons brandy (60ml)
3 tablespoons Lyle's Golden Syrup
1 cinnamon stick, about 8cm long
1/4 teaspoon ground ginger
good grate of nutmeg
2 fresh peeled and segmented satsumas
500ml lemonade

Stud the orange with the cloves, wrap in foil and roast in a medium oven (180C/350F/Gas 4) for 20 minutes. Meanwhile, put all the other ingredients into a large saucepan finally adding the roasted orange. Bring almost to the boil and then reduce the heat down to a very gentle simmer for about 20 minutes. Check for taste, temperature (you want it warm not too hot) and add more golden syrup if needed.

When ready to serve remove the pan from the heat and ladle the warming aromatic wine into suitable glasses (with a teaspoon in each to avoid cracking the glass).

**ASK YOUR GROCER
FOR IT!**
AN ADVERTISEMENT FROM THE 1900s

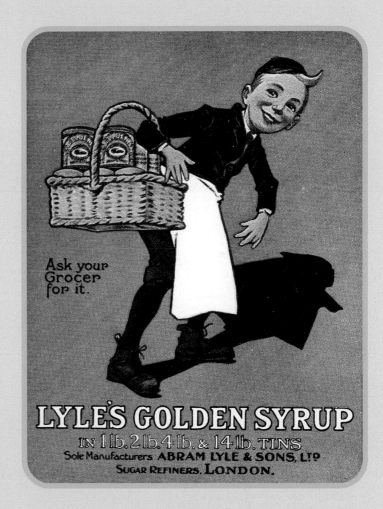

MALAYSIAN KING PRAWNS WITH STICKY WILD RICE

This creates a wonderful combination of fiery, salty prawns with the sweetness of the sticky rice and the freshness of the coriander.

SERVES 4

For the chilli paste
3 birds eye chillies, roughly chopped
1 small shallot, sliced
1 small stalk of lemongrass, finely sliced
1 clove garlic, finely chopped
2 teaspoons lime juice
1 teaspoon fresh chopped coriander stems (reserving leaves
    for garnish later)
1 teaspoon coarse sea salt
1 tablespoon Lyle's Golden Syrup

400g raw peeled king prawns
400ml coconut milk mixed with 400ml water
150g wild rice
100g basmati rice
1 tablespoons Lyle's Golden Syrup

Pound all the chilli paste ingredients with a pestle and mortar or whizz using a hand blender to make a thick paste.

Put the coconut milk and water into a pan and bring to the boil. Add the wild rice and simmer for 30 minutes. Next add the basmati rice (you may need to add a little boiling water to ensure there is enough liquid) and simmer for 10 minutes. When the rice is cooked drain it without rinsing, return it to the pan and stir in the golden syrup then leave covered to keep warm.

Put the chilli paste into a frying pan and heat gently. Add the raw prawns and cook for 3–4 minutes until they turn pretty pink and are well coated with the chilli paste.

Arrange the sticky rice in warmed serving bowls, lay the prawns on top, scatter with coriander leaves and serve.

RHUBARB & SYRUP CREAM FLAN

Light, fluffy and creamy with vibrant sweet rhubarb.

SERVES 6–8

300g rhubarb, cut into 4cm lengths
2 tablespoons Lyle's Golden Syrup
butter for greasing
100ml milk
150ml double cream
100g caster sugar
3 medium free-range eggs
25g plain flour
pinch salt
1 tablespoon Amaretto
icing sugar to dust

Preheat the oven to 190C/375F/Gas 5.

Cook the rhubarb and golden syrup in a pan very gently until the rhubarb gets to the al dente stage. (This means only just tender). Using a slotted spoon place the rhubarb in a buttered 25cm flan dish, spreading it out evenly over the base.

Whisk together all the remaining ingredients, except the icing sugar, until thick and creamy. Pour the mixture over the rhubarb and bake in the centre of the oven for 25–30 minutes. When ready the surface of the flan will have risen with a more golden border around the edge of the dish. When removed from the oven the flan will sink in the centre – don't worry this is meant to happen as the egg custard sets.

Dust with icing sugar and serve as spoonfuls of warm flan or allow to cool and cut into slices.

PERFECTION!

TRIPLE-MICHELIN-STARRED CHEF HESTON BLUMENTHAL, SEARCHING FOR THE ULTIMATE INGREDIENTS WITH WHICH TO MAKE TREACLE TART, DECLARED THERE TO BE NO SUPERIOR ALTERNATIVE TO LYLE'S GOLDEN SYRUP!

ROAST CHICKEN WITH GARLIC & LEMON

I love the fusion of chicken and lemon; add fresh garlic, syrup and wine for a marriage made in heaven.

SERVES 4–6

1 medium to large free-range chicken
4 unwaxed lemons (if you can't get unwaxed use regular
   ones but scrub the skin well under hot water)
8 cloves garlic, unpeeled
6 shallots, peeled
4 good sprigs fresh thyme
2 tablespoons olive oil
175ml white wine
2 tablespoons Lyle's Golden Syrup
sea salt and black pepper

Preheat the oven to 150C/300F/Gas 2.

Cut the chicken up into small joints and large chunks and put into a roasting pan. Cut each lemon (still with the skin on) into 8 chunks and add to the chicken together with the garlic cloves and shallots. Break up the thyme sprigs, discarding any woody stems and scatter over the chicken then spoon in the olive oil and massage everything well together with your hands so that all the ingredients are mixed.

Pour the wine over everything and then drizzle with the syrup. Season with sea salt and lots of freshly ground black pepper. Cover the roasting pan very tightly with foil and then put in the oven for $1^{1}/_{2}$ hours.

Remove the foil and turn the oven up to 220C/425F/Gas 7. Make sure all the chicken pieces are skin side up and then return to the oven for another 20 minutes or until all the edges of the lemons, shallots and garlic are dark golden brown.

Serve straight from the oven to the centre of the table for your guests to tuck into.

LYLE'S LEGEND & LORE

GOLDEN OLDIE

IN 2007, GUINNESS WORLD RECORDS recognised Lyle's Golden Syrup as having the world's oldest branding (packaging). The famous green and gold tin has remained virtually unchanged since 1885! The Lyle's arch and lion-and-bees logo have dressed the tin for all of that time and have been familiar to generation after generation of families in Britain and throughout the world. Lyle's can boast to being older than Coca Cola (1886), Marmite (1902), and Cadbury's Dairy Milk (1905)! In 2008, at 125 years of age, and to celebrate this milestone, the tin undergoes a special birthday makeover with limited-edition gold tins hitting the shelves.

SYRUP SPONGE PUDDING

There is comfort food and comfort food and believe me this is just the best totally irresistible and most indulgent comfort food in the planet.

SERVES 4

75g softened unsalted butter, plus a little for greasing
75g soft light brown sugar
2 large eggs, beaten
100g self-raising flour
1 level teaspoon baking powder
1 tablespoon milk

For the sauce
3 tablespoons Lyle's Golden Syrup plus extra to serve
4 tablespoons freshly squeezed orange juice

Butter the inside of a 1 pint pudding basin.

Take a large mixing bowl and beat together the butter and sugar until it is really soft and light. An electric whisk is ideal for this. Gradually add the beaten eggs, sieve in the flour and baking powder and finally add the milk. Beat the mixture well until it is thoroughly blended and you have a dropping consistency. Pour the mixture into the basin, making a nice level surface with the back of a spoon.

Line a sheet of foil with a sheet of greaseproof paper and fold to make a pleat in the centre – this will allow for expansion as the pudding rises. Cover the basin with the lined foil and wrap around the rim firmly. Then tie round with a piece of string to secure the foil in place. Stand the basin in a steamer or in a pan of simmering water, put the lid on the pan and steam for $1\frac{1}{2}$ hours, keeping an eye on the water level and topping up with boiling water as necessary.

Combine the sauce ingredients in a small pan and heat gently. When the pudding is cooked, remove from the pan, unwrap and ease the edges of the pudding away from the basin with a palette knife. Turn out onto a warmed plate and spoon over loads of golden syrup, which will soak into the sponge. Finally pour the warm orange syrup over the pudding and serve.

ENDIVE, MANGO & DATE SALAD

The combination of the bitter endive and the sweet Golden Syrup makes this a bright, fresh salad perfect for anytime but especially good with cold roast game.

SERVES 6

For the salad
1 endive (French, curly, slightly bitter lettuce; note that chicory is also called endive but for this use the full-blown lettuce)
1 fresh mango
1 red pepper, de-seeded, quartered and finely sliced
4 ready to eat dates
handful of parsley, chopped

For the dressing
(these ingredients should be at room temperature)
1 heaped teaspoon Dijon mustard
$1/2$ teaspoon celery salt
good grind of black pepper
1 tablespoon Lyle's Golden Syrup
2 tablespoons red wine vinegar
2 tablespoons olive oil
3 tablespoons walnut oil

Separate the leaves of the endive, putting aside any that are not fresh, wash the remainder in cold water and shake dry. Now place the leaves around the edge of the salad bowl working your way inwards in a way I can only describe as rebuilding the lettuce. Depending on the size you will probably only need to use about half of the lettuce.

Using a small sharp knife take the mango and slide the knife into the flesh working round the stone, first from one side and then the other. Pull the two sides apart and discard the stone. Now criss-cross the flesh inside the mango halves with the knife and turn inside out and voilá you have great little cubes of mango. Carefully cut them from the outer skin and pile them into the centre of the endive 'flower' followed by the colourful slithers of red pepper and topped with sliced dates.

In a blender put the mustard, salt and pepper, golden syrup, vinegar and olive oil and blitz until the mixture thickens. Finally stir in the walnut oil but do not blitz again. Drizzle the vinaigrette with a small ladle around the lettuce and then moving in over the mango and peppers, adding a flourish of parsley to complete the dish.

CARIBBEAN BANANA BREAD

Picture the scene – golden beaches, swaying palm trees, a Coconut Kiss cocktail and this scrummy banana bread – heaven was never this good!

MAKES A 450G LOAF

250g plain white flour
$^1/_2$ teaspoon salt
1 teaspoon baking powder
100g unsalted butter or margarine
2 medium free-range eggs
2 tablespoons Lyle's Golden Syrup
100g caster sugar
1 large, ripe banana
1 tablespoon shelled pecan nuts, roughly chopped

Preheat the oven to 180C/350F/Gas 4.

Prepare a 1lb loaf tin by buttering and flouring it and cutting a piece of baking parchment to fit the base.

Sieve the flour, salt and baking powder into a large bowl and then gradually add the butter or margarine in small cubes, rubbing the mixture with your fingertips until you have the look of fairly coarse breadcrumbs.

Whisk the eggs in a separate bowl, then add in the golden syrup and sugar and carry on whisking until the mixture is really creamy. Roughly mash the banana and add it to the egg mixture together with the pecan nuts.

Fold the flour into the egg, syrup and banana and combine until the ingredients are well mixed. Transfer the mixture into the loaf tin and spread evenly with the back of a spoon.

Bake in the centre of the hot oven for 30 minutes, or until golden and cooked through. Remove from the oven, allow to cool a little so that the bread comes away easily from the side of the tin and then turn out onto a cooling rack, carefully removing the paper from the base. This banana bread is delicious eaten warm – especially with an extra drizzle of golden syrup.

SILVER SCREEN, GOLDEN SYRUP

**DID YOU KNOW...
MAKE-UP ARTISTS FROM THE
WORLD OF TV AND FILM
COMBINE LYLE'S GOLDEN
SYRUP WITH RED FOOD
COLOURING TO CREATE
FAKE BLOOD?**

RED CABBAGE BRAISED WITH ORANGE & CRANBERRIES

Rich in colour, texture and flavour this long, slow cook vegetable dish will tease out the taste buds, it will sizzle up the sausages, perk up the pork, liven up the lamb and its easy to make – what more could you want?

MAKES ABOUT 8 PORTIONS

50g unsalted butter
2 red onions, peeled and sliced
1 medium red cabbage, (700–800g) finely sliced with outer
    leaves removed
200g fresh cranberries
$\frac{1}{2}$ teaspoon ground cinnamon
$\frac{1}{2}$ teaspoon ground ginger
5 tablespoons Lyle's Golden Syrup
4 tablespoons red wine vinegar
juice and zest of a large orange
salt and pepper

This is worth making as a whole and freezing in batches for future use.

In a large heavy based saucepan melt the butter, add the onions and let them sweat gently for 10 minutes with the lid on. Turn up the heat, add the red cabbage, mix well with the onions, cover the pan again and reduce to a simmer for a further 10 minutes.

Combine all the remaining ingredients in a bowl and add to the pan, stirring to mix everything together. Cover the pan; turn the heat down to the lowest setting and cook for 1 hour. Check and stir occasionally – there should be sufficient liquid for the cabbage to poach but you can always add a splash more orange juice if required.

Remove the saucepan lid, season with a little salt and pepper and continue cooking for a further 15 minutes, or until there is very little liquid left in the pan which means it is ready to serve.

Red cabbage goes especially well with any roast meats or casseroles and makes a rich and colourful display on the plate.

IT COMES IN BIG TINS TOO!
A SHOW CARD FROM THE 1900s

SUNSHINE FRUITS IN ORANGE, MINT & YOGHURT

Fantastic summer fruit fusion – even when the skies are grey this taste of summer will bring a smile to your taste buds.

SERVES 4

2 peaches – obviously in season is best but in any event
   select them from a good fruiterer
16 fresh strawberries
4 dessertspoons blackcurrants (you can use tinned and
   drained)
zest and juice of $\frac{1}{2}$ orange
1 tablespoon Lyle's Golden Syrup
4 tablespoons thick natural yoghurt, plus extra for garnish
4 mint leaves, chopped and 4 mint sprigs for garnish
1 teaspoon crushed pink peppercorns

Halve the peaches, remove the stone and cut each half into thin segments.

Hull the strawberries and slice in half, top and tail the currants if using fresh.

Place the zest and orange juice into a bowl with the juice of the orange; add the golden syrup, the 4 tablespoons of yoghurt and the chopped mint leaves. Mix this dressing thoroughly. Now drizzle the yoghurt mixture over the fruit, sprinkle with the crushed pink peppercorns and place one final teaspoon of yoghurt on the side, onto which you can place a sprig of mint and then serve.

HERRINGS WITH SWEET DILL MUSTARD

This dill mustard sauce is equally good with gravlax or smoked salmon.

SERVES 4

4 herrings, filleted
400ml white wine vinegar
200ml water
1 cinnamon stick, about 5cm
1 teaspoon allspice berries
1 teaspoon black peppercorns
4 whole cloves
1 large onion, finely sliced
2 tablespoons Lyle's Golden Syrup

For the sweet dill mustard
2 tablespoons Dijon mustard
1 tablespoon white wine vinegar
90ml whipping cream
1 tablespoon Lyle's Golden Syrup
2 tablespoons chopped fresh dill plus a few fronds for
   garnish

Slice each herring fillet into 3 diagonal strips.

Put the vinegar, water, spices, onion and syrup into a pan and bring to the boil. Simmer for 15 minutes and then add the herring strips, skin side up, simmering gently for a further 15 minutes.

Allow to cool then tip the herring mixture into a shallow dish, remove the cinnamon stick, then cover and refrigerate overnight.

About an hour before serving whisk together all the sweet dill mustard ingredients, except the dill, in a small bowl until it is thick and creamy. Stir in the chopped dill and leave in the fridge to infuse all the lovely flavours.

Now lift the herring fillets and onions out of the dish with a slotted spoon (leaving the spices behind) onto serving plates and spoon over the mustard dressing. Scatter the remaining dill sprigs over the top. A crispy salad and chunks of warm crusty bread, or better still pumpernickel, are all you need to enjoy this perfect lunch.

BROWN BREAD GOLDEN SYRUP ICE CREAM

I love this ice cream – a really easy dessert to make. Dress it to impress, by topping with sliced, seasonal fruit.

MAKES ABOUT 1 LITRE

100g brown breadcrumbs
50g soft brown sugar
400ml double cream
1 tablespoon dark rum
2 tablespoons Lyle's Golden Syrup
50g icing sugar

Preheat the oven to 180C/350F/Gas 4.

Mix together the breadcrumbs and the sugar and bake in the oven for 10 minutes, stirring a couple of times then remove and leave aside to cool.

Whisk the double cream until fairly firm and then add the rum, fold in the golden syrup and sieved icing sugar. Pour into a suitable plastic container and freeze for 2 hours.

Remove from the freezer and beat the ice cream well for a couple of minutes. Finally fold in the baked breadcrumbs and sugar. Return to the freezer for a further 2–3 hours or overnight.

LYLE'S LOVES...

SPONGE PUDDING

THERE ARE MORE VARIETIES of sponge pudding than you can shake a tin of syrup at (and nothing crowns one better!), but did you know...

In a 2003 poll carried out by *BBC Good Food* magazine, sponge pudding was voted one of the best five school dinners ever. And the worst? Tapioca, perhaps better remembered as 'frog-spawn'!

There's no greater British institution dedicated to preserving the Great British culinary tradition of sponge pudding and all its brothers and sisters – than the Cotswold-based Pudding Club. It's a society that meets several times every month at the Three Ways House Hotel to indulge in a 7-course pudding extravaganza! The hotel even has a room called the 'Syrup Sponge Room' inspired by Lyle's Golden Syrup, with a bed created to look like a sponge pudding, and other Lyle's paraphernalia dotting the walls.

STRAWBERRY & BLUEBERRY SMOOTHIE

Big on nutrition, short on preparation time – this makes for perfect mornings.

SERVES 2

250g natural yoghurt
225g strawberries, hulled
75g blueberries
1–2 tablespoons Lyle's Golden Syrup (according to your morning taste buds)
4 ice cubes
2 sprigs fresh mint

(Seasonal fruit will vary in sweetness so when blitzing the ingredients start with the lesser amount of syrup and increase it as necessary.)

This couldn't be simpler. Simply blitz together the yoghurt, fruit, syrup and ice for about 30 seconds.

Pour into a tall glass and garnish with a sprig of mint. For an extra wholesome start to the day you can sprinkle a spoonful of your favourite muesli on top and serve with a long spoon as well.

PURVEYORS OF ONLY THE FINEST GOODS

A 19TH-CENTURY EMPORIUM SELLING LYLE'S GOLDEN SYRUP

ROAST LAMB WITH CRUSHED ROSEMARY GLAZE

The Golden Syrup married to the rosemary really adds a rich and exuberant flavour to this favourite family roast!

SERVES 3–4

1 whole bulb of garlic with the top cut off
olive oil
coarse sea salt
1 whole orange cut into 8 chunks
3 good stems of rosemary
$^1/_2$ leg of lamb (around 1kg)
2 tablespoons Lyle's Golden Syrup
black pepper

Heat the oven to 200C/400F/Gas 6.

Put the garlic bulb into a roasting dish, drizzle with olive oil and sprinkle with sea salt. Place the dish in the oven and roast for 20 minutes. Remove and cool the garlic until cool enough to handle and then squeeze out the soft cloves into the roasting dish. Add to this the orange chunks and the leaves plucked from the rosemary sprigs crushed with the back of a spoon to release their pungent flavour.

Using a sharp knife cut insertions in the raw lamb like a criss-cross. Place the lamb in an open plastic bag and add all the ingredients from the roasting dish. Seal up the bag and shake the lot. Place in the fridge for at least one hour shaking as before every 10 minutes. You can do this the night before you want your roast, if preferred.

Keep the oven ready at 180C/350F/Gas 4. Place the leg of lamb in a roasting dish and coat with golden syrup spreading it into the slits. Tuck the orange segments in under the joint and massage the rosemary and garlic into the lamb emptying any juicy bits from the marinade bag into the dish. Season with plenty of black pepper.

You will need to cook the joint for 20 minutes per 1lb (450g) plus 20 minutes. This will leave the outside crispy and the inside still slightly pink. Baste the joint a few times to keep the full flavour of the juices infusing into the lamb.

When cooked remove and leave to rest for 10 minutes covered loosely with kitchen foil. Strain the remaining juices to add to your gravy and your rosemary roast lamb is ready to enjoy.

CINNAMON GINGERBREAD HEARTS

Did Elvis Presley sing about gingerbread hearts? You will when you've made these.

MAKES 15–20 HEARTS

300g plain flour, plus extra for kneading
$^1/_2$ teaspoon salt
1 teaspoon baking powder
1 teaspoon ground ginger
1$^1/_2$ teaspoons ground cinnamon
$^1/_4$ teaspoon freshly grated nutmeg
60g softened butter
100g caster sugar
6 tablespoons Lyle's Golden Syrup
1 egg yolk

Preheat the oven to 180C/350F/Gas 4.

Sieve the flour, salt, baking powder and spices into a bowl.

In a larger bowl beat together the butter, sugar and syrup until you have a stiff but creamy mixture. Add the egg yolk and beat really well. Now gently blend in the flour mixture until you have a firm dough.

On a well floured board, roll out the dough to about 1cm thick. If it feels too sticky add extra flour so that you can knead the mixture into a fairly firm dough. Chill for 30 minutes.

Using a heart shaped biscuit cutter cut out as many as the dough will allow. Re-roll the dough to use up the remainder for more hearts. Place them on a greased baking tray, allowing 2–3cm between each biscuit, as they will expand, and cook in the centre of the oven for 8–10 minutes until just golden.

Cool on a wire rack and then store in an airtight container. These biscuits are delicious served with Baked Apples with Prunes in Cinnamon Syrup (page 8).

At Christmas time it's great fun to hang these on the tree. As the hearts are just beginning to cool carefully pierce a hole through with a skewer near the top of the biscuit, wide enough to squeeze a thin ribbon through. When cool you can hang them on the Christmas tree.

DELIVERING THE GOODS
A SELECTION OF VINTAGE VEHICLES

ABRAM LYLE & SONS Ltd
PURVEYORS OF GOLDEN SYRUP
..BY APPOINTMENT TO.
HIS MAJESTY THE KING.
LONDON

LYLE'S GOLDEN SYRUP
ABRAM LYLE & SONS Limited
SUGAR REFINERS
TWO POUNDS NET.

NOTICE.
Owing to the requirements of the Ministry of Munitions with a view to economy in the use of tin plate, we are compelled to adopt this substitute for our usual lever lid tins. There is no change in the quality or weight of the contents.
ABRAM LYLE & SONS, Ltd.
LYLE'S GOLDEN SYRUP IS GUARANTEED PURE.

THE WARTIME MAKESHIFT

THE CARDBOARD TIN
THE TIN HAS CHANGED LITTLE IN 125 YEARS, THOUGH THE CARDBOARD EDITION ABOVE WAS PUT INTO PRODUCTION DURING THE YEARS OF THE FIRST WORLD WAR WHEN METAL WAS IN SHORT SUPPLY.

THE ANNIVERSARY TIN
TO CELEBRATE 125 YEARS, LIMITED-EDITION GOLD ANNIVERSARY TINS (LEFT) ARE PRODUCED TO MARK THE INCREDIBLE MILESTONE IN UNDERSTATED ELEGANCE.

FRUIT & NUT MUFFINS WITH DRAMBUIE CREAM

Delightful, little, nut-brown individual pudding cakes fused with spices and served with Drambuie cream – not a calorie in sight!

MAKES 9–12 CAKES

200g self-raising flour
2 teaspoons baking powder
$^1/_2$ teaspoon salt
$^1/_2$ teaspoon ground cinnamon
$^1/_4$ teaspoon ground nutmeg
100g caster sugar
60g chopped mixed fruit
50g walnuts, finely chopped
2 tablespoons Lyle's Golden Syrup
50g melted butter
200ml milk
1 egg

For the Drambuie Cream
400ml double cream
1 tablespoon Lyle's Golden Syrup
2 tablespoons Drambuie

You will need a non-stick muffin tin for this recipe.

Preheat the oven to 220C/425F/Gas 7.

Into a large bowl sieve the flour, baking powder, salt, cinnamon and nutmeg and then add the sugar and stir in the dried fruit and nuts

In a separate bowl add the golden syrup to the melted butter and mix well with a fork. Add the milk and egg and whisk again.

Gradually pour the milk and egg mix into the flour and stir until all the ingredients are combined into a lumpy mixture – do not overwork it. Spoon the mixture into the muffin cups to about two thirds full and bake in the centre of the hot oven for 15 minutes or until the muffins are well risen and golden.

Whisk the cream until really thick and then stir in the syrup and Drambuie. Serve with the muffins for a perfect pud.

LYLE'S LEGEND & LORE

THE LION & THE BEES

The illustration of a dead lion with bees swarming round its head has adorned the tin for almost all of the syrup's 125 years. The illustration has been modified slightly over time, and refers to a passage from The Book of Judges in which Samson kills a lion. Samson later notices that bees have formed a honeycomb in the carcass of the dead animal, and muses, 'Out of the eater came forth meat and out of the strong came forth sweetness'. Lyle was a deeply religious man, and the second half of the passage obviously appealed and must have struck Lyle as a fitting proverb for his syrup – within his strong metal gold-and-green tin lay the most wonderful sweetness of all.

COURGETTES IN WHITE WINE & GOLDEN SYRUP

Courgettes, when in season, are plentiful and cheap but can hide their taste. This recipe brings out the best in any courgette or marrow and works equally well with sliced, cooked beetroot.

SERVES 4

500g courgettes
1 medium onion
1 clove garlic
1 tablespoon olive oil
200ml dry white wine
salt and black pepper
1 tablespoon Lyle's Golden Syrup
12 seedless grapes, halved

Top, tail and peel the courgettes and cut slices on the diagonal about 1cm thick.

Peel the onion and cut it in half. Lay each half face down and slice into thin slithers. Peel the clove of garlic and finely dice.

In a deep frying pan gently heat the olive oil and fry the onion and garlic for 2–3 minutes until soft and transparent – you don't want them crispy. Now lay the slices of courgette on top. Turn up the heat to medium high and pour over the white wine. Season with salt and plenty of freshly milled black pepper and let the courgettes gently poach for 8–10 minutes turning several times until the liquid has almost gone. Drizzle the golden syrup over the courgettes, turn once or twice to glaze. Finally toss in the grapes, just enough to warm them, and serve as an easy lunch or to accompany fresh grilled fish or white meat.

THAI FRIED BANANAS

A classic Thai dish – a sensational fusion of sun-drenched bananas, coconut milk and golden syrup.

SERVES 4

For the batter
150g rice flour
160ml water
50g dessicated coconut
1 tablespoon plain flour
1 tablespoon Lyle's Golden Syrup
1 level tablespoon sesame seeds
1 teaspoon baking powder
pinch salt

corn oil for deep-frying
4 slightly green bananas

For the sauce
400ml tin of coconut milk
1 tablespoon Lyle's Golden Syrup

In a large bowl whisk together all the batter ingredients and leave to stand.

Pour the tin of coconut milk into a saucepan over a fairly high heat and reduce the milk by half (keep the tin as an easy measure). Reduce the heat, add the golden syrup and stir well and then keep the sauce warm until you are ready for it.

Heat the oil in a wok or deep fat fryer. A good hint here is to toss a small cube of bread into the oil and if it sizzles immediately then the oil is hot enough. Peel the bananas and cut each one in half lengthways and then in half widthways. Dip the banana pieces into the coconut batter and then deep fry them until just golden – about 2 minutes on each side. Remove with a slotted spoon, drain on kitchen paper and keep warm.

In 4 warmed bowls stack the fried banana pieces and drizzle with the thick creamy coconut milk. Serve immediately.

CRYSTAL TIPS

IF YOUR GOLDEN SYRUP HAS CRYSTALS IN IT, FEAR NOT! YOU CAN EASILY REMOVE THEM BY STANDING THE OPEN TIN IN A PAN OF HOT WATER AND STIRRING UNTIL THE CRYSTALS DISSOLVE.

PORK MEDALLIONS WITH SWEET MUSTARD CRUST

Succulent pork fillet, sweet golden syrup, a keen mustard bite and tart apple sauce makes this dish a favourite for kids and adults alike for lunches and suppers.

SERVES 4

600g pork fillet
2 teaspoons ready made English mustard
2 tablespoons Lyle's Golden Syrup
2 tablespoons ready-made apple sauce
good grind of black pepper
100g fresh breadcrumbs
sunflower oil for frying
parsley, chopped for scattering
wedges of lemon

Cut the pork fillet into 1cm wide slices and then placing the slices – now called medallions – between two sheets of clingfilm pummel them with a steak hammer or rolling pin until they are about half the thickness and twice as wide. This also tenderises the meat.

In a small mixing bowl place the mustard, golden syrup, apple sauce and black pepper and mix well together. Put the breadcrumbs in a shallow dish.

Pick up each medallion and spread one side with the sauce mixture then press into the breadcrumbs. Repeat with the other side so that the medallions are completely coated – this can get quite messy – then set aside on a plate covered with greaseproof paper. Chill these in a refrigerator for 1 hour to set the crust.

Heat the oil in a frying pan, and sauté the medallions in batches for 3–4 minutes on each side until they are a glorious golden colour. Drain on kitchen paper and keep warm while you cook the remainder.

Serve with a scattering of parsley and wedges of lemon.

LYLE'S LOVES...
ICE CREAM

ICE CREAM AND SYRUP are a marriage made in heaven. For precision drizzles, why not try squirting from a Lyle's Squeezy Syrup bottle? Ice cream pre-dates our beloved syrup by many, many years. Indeed, legend has it that...

In Roman times, Emperor Nero might have come up with the precursor to ice-cream. He used to send slaves up into the mountains to collect snow and ice with which to make flavoured ices!

The ice cream cone was invented by a New York City ice cream vendor in 1896, to prevent customers from stealing his serving glasses!

GOLDEN SYRUP BEIGNETS

Serve these delicious beignets with good hot coffee in the morning for a perfectly indulgent start to the day.

MAKES 10–12 'LITTLE DOUGHNUTS'

120ml water
60g unsalted butter
1 tablespoon Lyle's Golden Syrup
$\frac{1}{2}$ teaspoon salt
75g plain flour
3 medium free-range eggs
2 teaspoons vanilla extract
caster sugar to dust

Combine the water, butter, syrup and salt in a saucepan and bring to the boil. Remove the pan from the heat; add the flour and stir like mad until it all comes together and looks a little shiny. Continue to cook and stir for 2–3 minutes and you will find that the mixture comes away from the side of the pan. Transfer the mixture to a bowl, allow to cool a little and then add the eggs, one at a time, beating each one in by hand for a couple of minutes, finally adding the vanilla.

Heat a deep fat fryer to 190C/375F and dip a ladle into the oil to coat. Drop a good tablespoon of the batter into the ladle and carefully lower the ladle into the oil. Turn the ladle to release the beignet and repeat with more of the batter, frying 4–5 beignets at a time until puffy and golden all over. Drain on kitchen paper and dust with caster sugar. Your beignets should be crispy on the outside and soft and yielding in the middle.

QUAIL ROASTED IN MADEIRA WITH BACON-WRAPPED FIGS

The texture of the figs and the opulence of Madeira wrapped around the richness of quail and bacon makes this a glorious dinner party dish.

SERVES 2

20g unsalted butter
4 oven ready quail
2 tablespoons Lyle's Golden Syrup
1 teaspoon mixed dried herbs
freshly ground black pepper
4 bay leaves
12 rashers streaky bacon
vegetable oil
2 fresh figs
200ml Madeira wine
1 teaspoon plain flour
handful black grapes, halved

Preheat the oven to 200C/400F/Gas 6.

Divide the butter into 4, put a knob inside each quail and tie up the legs with string. Drizzle each bird with a teaspoon of golden syrup, scatter with the mixed herbs, season with pepper and lay a bay leaf on top of each.

Take 8 of the bacon rashers, stretch them out with a knife and wrap each way around the quail in the shape of a cross. Place the birds in an oiled roasting tin and roast in the oven for 15 minutes.

Carefully, using a sharp knife, peel and quarter the figs. Stretch out the remaining bacon rashers, cut each into 2 and wrap around each piece of fig. Remove the quail from the oven and turn it up to 220C/425F/Gas 7. Remove the bacon from the birds, leaving it in the tin for flavour, and add the wrapped figs. Drizzle the quail with the remaining golden syrup and add $3/4$ of the Madeira to the roasting tin. Return the quail to the oven for a further 15 minutes.

When the birds are cooked remove them from the roasting tin using 2 forks upending each as you do so to drain out any buttery juices from inside the quail. Put them onto a warm dish to rest for at least 5 minutes, together with the wrapped figs.

When the juices in the roasting tin have cooled a little sprinkle in the flour and add the rest of the Madeira. Put the tin on top of the stove over a gentle heat; stir all the juices to thicken into syrupy gravy and throw in the grapes to warm. Arrange the quail and figs on warm serving plates and spoon over the gravy and grapes to serve.

RUM & GOLDEN SYRUP HOT FRUIT SALAD

This is an excellent dessert to serve as a final flourish for an informal supper party – big on texture, colour and flavour.

SERVES 6

4 tablespoons Lyle's Golden Syrup
2 tablespoons Malibu
2 good sprigs fresh mint
1 medium pineapple
3 greengages or red plums
2 peaches
2 bananas

Preheat the oven to 180C/350F/Gas 4.

In a small pan gently heat the syrup and Malibu until well mixed and runny. Remove from the heat and add finely sliced leaves from the mint sprigs, reserving a few for later. Leave aside to infuse.

Next prepare the fruit using a large shallow dish. Peel the pineapple leaving the leaves still attached and cut into 6 segments lengthways. Wrap the leaves in foil to avoid them burning. Cut the plums in half and remove the stones. Stone the peaches and cut into quarters. Peel the bananas and cut each into 3 large diagonal slices. Put all the fruit into the dish and pour the rum syrup over everything.

Preheat the grill to high. (If you have a ridged griddle pan you can use this on top of the cooker instead of grilling and you will get gorgeously scorched lines on your fruit as you would on the barbecue). Start with the pineapple, then plums, and then peaches and lay the fruit pieces, flesh side down, on the grill rack or griddle turning once or twice until browned. Transfer the fruits to a baking dish and put into the oven as you go. Cook in the oven for 10 minutes and then lastly grill or griddle the banana, (the softest fruit) and add it to the oven dish to cook for a further 5 minutes.

Unwrap the foil from the pineapple leaves and serve the golden fruits drizzled with the remaining juices and garnished with the reserved mint leaves.

LYLE'S LEGEND & LORE

DRIZZLY DARES

LYLE'S GOLDEN SYRUP is perfect over so many things, but have you tried a drizzle over the following? Go on, give it a go!

• Drizzle over fruit before grilling – it's fantastic on apples and raisins and on peach halves. It's also great on banana and cinnamon.

• Watch it sink into the tiny holes of lovely hot crumpets for a soft, sweet treat.

• Swirl it into your pasta sauce to help take the sharpness off tomatoes.

• Simplest of all, lash it over hot buttered toast for a quick taste of the divine!

GREEK BEEF STIFADO WITH BABY ONIONS

All around the world you'll find stews with a regional influence. This Greek-inspired dish is slow in cooking and big in flavour.

SERVES 4

50ml olive oil
500g braising steak, cut into largish cubes
250g small cooking onions, peeled (plunge them into boiling
   water for a few minutes prior to make peeling easier)
100ml red wine
2 tablespoons Lyle's Golden Syrup
1 tablespoon red wine vinegar
3 cloves garlic, roughly chopped
400g tin peeled, chopped tomatoes
2 teaspoons dried oregano
2 bay leaves
1 cinnamon stick (about 6cm)
pinch grated nutmeg
pinch ground allspice
salt and freshly ground black pepper
500ml good beef stock

Heat about half of the olive oil in a heavy based saucepan and seal the beef in batches, lifting it out with a slotted spoon and keeping aside.

Add the remaining oil into the pan. Sauté the onions gently keeping them whole, until they are lightly golden and just softening. Remove them from the pan with a slotted spoon and keep aside. Add the red wine to the pan followed by the golden syrup and the vinegar, scraping all the good bits from the bottom of the pan and cook for a few more minutes.

Return the meat to the pan and add the garlic, tomatoes, herbs and spices then season with the salt and pepper. Finally add enough beef stock to make a rich gravy. Cook over a very low heat for 1 hour.

Next add the onions and continue cooking for a further $1\frac{1}{2}$ hours, with an occasional stir, until the meat is meltingly tender. When the stifado is cooked remove it from the heat and leave covered for about half an hour.

It should be served warm not piping hot and traditionally with fresh crusty bread and salad. I once had stifado served with crumbled feta cheese on top, which gave a delicious salty contrast to the sweetness of the dish.

GRANNY SMITH TOFFEE APPLES

This traditional treat has long been part of the autumn festivals like Hallowe'en and Guy Fawkes – this recipe is perfect for kids of all ages.

MAKES 6 TOFFEE APPLES

6 Granny Smith apples
250g Demerara sugar
100ml water
$^1/_2$ teaspoon vinegar
2 tablespoons Lyle's Golden Syrup
25g butter
6 tablespoons unsalted peanuts, crushed

You will need 6 strong wooden skewers and ideally an extra pair of hands (or the kids) as the last stage of making these toffee apples happens very quickly.

Push a wooden skewer into each apple and set aside.

In a heavy based pan warm the sugar and water over a medium heat until all the grains have dissolved, swirling the pan rather than stirring the liquid. Do not use a high heat, as this will crystallise the liquid. Next add the vinegar, syrup and butter.

Bring the mixture up to the boil watching all the time (very important) without stirring until it reaches what is called the 'hard crack' stage. This is when half a teaspoon of the sugary mixture hardens into a ball when dropped in a bowl of cold water or sets hard on a very cold plate. The timing will vary according to your pan size and the temperature so just keep checking until it happens. Now you have toffee!

Prepare a tray with the crushed peanuts in and then holding the skewer dip each apple into the hot toffee, swirling it around to completely coat. Then immediately roll the toffee apple in the crushed peanuts for the outer coating and stand on a buttered baking tray. Repeat with the remaining apples.

If they are not to be eaten that day its best to wrap them in cellophane and they will keep in the fridge for several days.

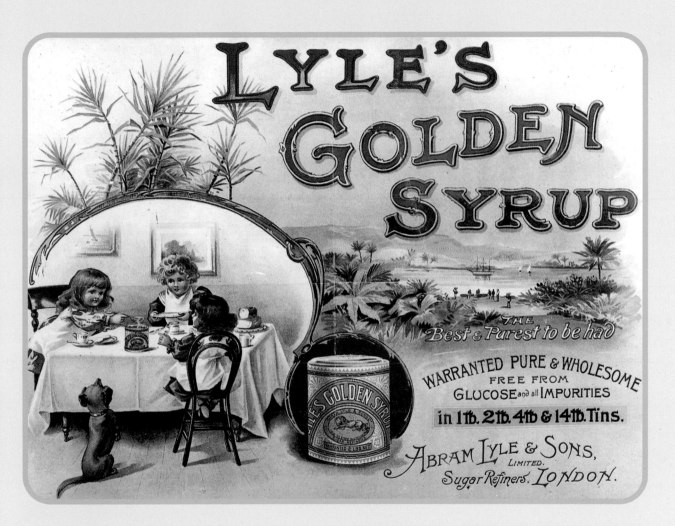

THE BEST & PUREST TO BE HAD!
AN ADVERTISEMENT FROM THE 1900s

FILLET STEAK STRIPS WITH SWEET GINGER STIR-FRY

If you want a dish to get your taste buds jumping just try this one – the acute flavours develop into a truly scrummy dish.

SERVES 2

Stir-fry sauce
5cm piece root ginger finely chopped
3 tablespoons dry sherry
1 tablespoon dark soy sauce
1 tablespoon Lyle's Golden Syrup
$\frac{1}{2}$ teaspoon Chinese five spice powder

2 fillet steaks (about 150g each)
1 tablespoon sesame oil
4 baby corn
100g sugar snap peas
1 small red pepper, deseeded and thinly sliced
handful of Chinese leaves or cabbage, shredded
1 teaspoon of toasted sesame seeds

Put all the stir-fry sauce ingredients into a shallow dish, mix well and add the steaks, turning them to coat thoroughly. Cover and leave to marinate for at least 1 hour.

Heat a lightly oiled griddle or heavy based frying pan until just beginning to smoke slightly. Remove the steaks from the marinade (keeping the juice for the stir-fry) and sear on both sides to seal in the juices. Cook for a further 3–4 minutes on each side. (If you prefer your steaks medium or more – cook on!) Remove from the pan and rest the steaks for 5 minutes, keeping them warm.

Meanwhile heat the sesame oil in a wok and add first the baby corn, then the sugar snaps, then the peppers and finally the Chinese leaves allowing each to cook for 2–3 minutes before adding the next. Cook everything quickly over a high heat. Add the remaining marinade to the wok, stir a few more times to heat through and your vegetables are ready to slide onto hot serving plates. Slice the steaks very thinly and arrange in a pile on top of the vegetables finishing with a final flourish of toasted sesame seeds.

FILO-TOPPED BOUGATSA PUDDING

Golden syrup makes a perfect partner to add a twist to this northern Greek speciality that I first tasted in the busy port of Thessaloniki.

MAKES 12 PORTIONS

900ml milk
100g caster sugar
1 vanilla bean, split in half lengthways
 (or 2 teaspoons vanilla extract)
75g semolina
100g unsalted butter, melted
4 large eggs, lightly beaten
500g ready made filo pastry (12 sheets)
2 tablespoons Lyle's Golden Syrup, warmed
1 tablespoon icing sugar
1 teaspoon ground cinnamon

Preheat the oven to 180C/350F/Gas 4

Place the milk, caster sugar and vanilla pod (or extract) into a saucepan and bring to the boil. Gradually add the semolina stirring all the time and then turn down the heat to medium. Cook for 10–12 minutes until the semolina begins to thicken, stirring continuously and then remove the pan from the heat. (If your semolina has gone lumpy, don't worry simply strain it through a sieve into another pan.) Allow to cool a little and then remove the vanilla pod (if using), scraping any seeds into the mixture. Add a tablespoon of the melted butter and the beaten eggs and stir into the semolina mixture, which will now be like a very thick custard.

Use a deep rectangular baking dish 25cm x 30cm or similar (about 10" x 12") and brush the bottom with melted butter. Lay 6 sheets of filo pastry in the dish, brushing each sheet with melted butter as you add it and allowing the pastry to overhang the sides of the dish. Pour the semolina custard into the dish. Cover with all but 1 of the remaining sheets of filo, brushing each with butter and this time drizzling each sheet with the warmed syrup as well. Fold in the overhanging pastry to encase the custard and fold the final sheet of filo in half and cut to fit the dish snugly on top. Using a pair of scissors (and this is a bit tricky) score the pastry into portions by just cutting through the last double layer of filo. Too much pressure, or cutting too deep will make the pastry move about and the custard leak out.

Bake in the middle of the oven for 10 minutes and then reduce the heat to 150C/300F/Gas 2 for a further 40 minutes. Remove from the oven, dust with the icing sugar and cinnamon (do not mix them together first as the colour contrast looks better) and pop it back in for 10 minutes. Remove and cool a little before serving warm with poached pears.

SICILIAN AUBERGINE & PINE NUT POLPETTES

Polpettes are delicious little bread crumbed balls found all over the Mediterranean with a multitude of sweet and savoury fillings, often both as in this Sicilian favourite.

MAKES 18 POLPETTES

1 medium aubergine
75g raisins, roughly chopped
50g toasted pine nuts
75g Pecorino cheese, finely grated (you could use Parmesan)
2 tablespoons Lyle's Golden Syrup
pinch grated nutmeg
little salt and a good grind of black pepper
2 free range eggs, beaten
200g fresh white breadcrumbs
flour for dusting
sunflower oil for frying

Peel and chunk the aubergine and put in a saucepan. Cover with water, bring to the boil and cook for 10 minutes. Drain through a sieve and then using a potato masher gently press out the remaining water and leave to cool.

Into a large bowl put the raisins, pine nuts, Pecorino, syrup and nutmeg and mix well together. Add the aubergine and mash into the fruity mixture with a wooden spoon. Then season with salt and pepper, add in $1/2$ of the beaten egg and about $2/3$ of the breadcrumbs until you have a consistency when mixed that will hold together when pressed – but not too sticky.

Pick up about a tablespoon of the mixture at a time and roll into balls about the size of a golf ball (weighing about 35g). Roll the balls in flour, dip into the remaining egg and then the breadcrumbs. Chill in the fridge for at least half an hour to set the coating.

Heat the oil in a frying pan or deep fat fryer to 190C/375F. Add the polpettes, turning them over as they cook for about 5 minutes or until golden brown and crispy. Drain on kitchen paper and serve just warm as a starter with a watercress and rocket salad.

TO BALDLY GO...

DID YOU KNOW... 'SYRUP' IS THE COCKNEY RHYMING SLANG FOR HAIRPIECE? SYRUP IS SHORT FOR SYRUP OF FIGS (WHICH RHYMES WITH WIG).

SWEET MARINATED LAMB, BACON AND APRICOT BROCHETTES

This is a whole flavour-bursting experience on a stick. Simple to create and loved by all – makes a perfect Saturday lunch with friends.

SERVES 4

2 tablespoons light soy sauce
1 teaspoon Dijon mustard
2 tablespoons Lyle's Golden Syrup
1 tablespoon lemon juice
2 shallots, finely diced
1 teaspoon dried mixed herbs
8 rashers smoked streaky bacon
600g lamb (neck fillet is ideal) cut into 24 slices
16 dried apricots (half-cooked or ready to eat)

In a bowl whisk together the soy, mustard, golden syrup and lemon juice and then add the shallots and herbs to make a marinade.

Cut each rasher of bacon in half and roll up into a sausage. Now alternately thread the lamb, bacon and apricots onto 8 bamboo skewers (3 lamb, 2 bacon and 2 apricots per skewer) and lay the brochettes out in a large, shallow dish. Pour the marinade over them, cover with clingfilm and leave for at least 2 hours, turning the brochettes in the juices once or twice.

Preheat the grill to medium hot, line the grill tray with foil, lay the brochettes on the rack and brush with loads of marinade. Cook for about 5 minutes on each side for pinkish lamb, or longer to your liking, basting with more marinade as they cook.

Serve with fluffy rice and a crunchy white cabbage and caper salad dressed only with olive oil, lemon juice, salt and pepper.

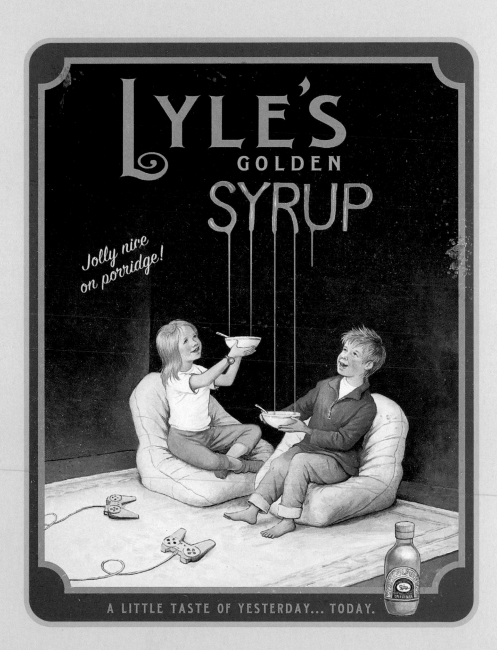

**CATCH IT
WHILST
YOU CAN!**
**A RETRO-STYLE
ADVERTISEMENT FROM
2005**

CARROT & CORIANDER SALAD WITH SWEET VINAIGRETTE

This is a very pretty and aromatic accompaniment rather than a main dish. It works exceedingly well with Mediterranean dishes like pasta and grilled fish.

SERVES 4–6

For the salad
2 large carrots, washed, peeled and grated
2 shallots, finely diced
25g fresh coriander, roughly chopped (must be fresh, not dried)
1 Cos style lettuce (Little Gem or Romaine are great)
100g pimento-stuffed olives, each one cut into 3 rings
1 teaspoon sesame seeds
coarse sea salt

For the dressing
1 heaped teaspoon wholegrain mustard
freshly milled black pepper
5 tablespoons olive oil
1 tablespoon Lyle's Golden Syrup
1 tablespoon cider vinegar or white wine vinegar
2 tablespoons orange juice

In a salad bowl place the grated carrots, diced shallots and coriander and mix together gently. In a blender put the mustard, black pepper, olive oil, golden syrup, vinegar and orange juice and whiz until it thickens. This can also be done by hand with a bowl and whisk, the only difference is that you will need to add the olive oil last and a little at a time as you whisk it so that it emulsifies nicely.

Drizzle the dressing over the salad and fold it together to coat everything.

Remove the leaves from the lettuce, wash in fresh water and dry. You will need 1 large leaf or 2–3 small ones per person. Arrange the leaves on serving plates and then fill with the dressed carrot and coriander salad. Scatter with the olive rings, arranging a few around the plate, sprinkle with the sesame seeds, a little coarse sea salt and serve.

LYLE'S LOVES...

MEAT

LYLE'S GOLDEN SYRUP is the perfect glaze for all sorts of meat. It gives a wonderfully sweet edge and adds fantastic depth and richness. Why not try it with the following:

ROAST JOINTS of Gammon (see page 18) and Lamb (see page 39).

CHICKEN WINGS
(Brush them lightly with syrup and then scatter chilli flakes over the top.)

SAUSAGES
(Serve then in hot dog rolls with fried onions that have been glazed with Golden Syrup.)

RICH PARKIN

Dating back to Victorian England, this spiced Yorkshire cake remains a firm favourite treat and so it should be.

150g self-raising flour
1 level teaspoon bicarbonate of soda
$^1/_2$ teaspoon ground cinnamon
1 teaspoon ground ginger
100g medium oatmeal
75g butter
150g Lyle's Golden Syrup
1 egg, beaten
2 tablespoons milk
75g candied peel, finely chopped
50g soft brown sugar

Preheat the oven to 150C/300F/Gas 2.

Butter and flour a 1lb loaf tin and cut a piece of baking parchment to fit the base.

Sift the flour, soda, cinnamon and ginger into a large bowl and then stir in the oatmeal.

In a small pan gently heat the butter and syrup until melted. Beat the egg with the milk. Gradually add the buttery syrup to the dry ingredients, stirring as you go to make a thick mixture. Then add the egg and milk, stirring until smooth and finally the candied peel and sugar. Pour the mixture into your prepared tin and bake in the centre of the oven for 1 hour.

The Parkin, which will keep moist for a considerable time in an airtight tin, should not be eaten until 24 hours after baking. This makes the perfect accompaniment to a brew of Yorkshire Tea.

GOLDEN SUNSET COCKTAIL

This is a big, fruity, cool cocktail to enjoy at all times of the day – just add that dash of Tequila as the sun goes down.

MAKES 4 TALL GLASSES

4 tablespoons Lyle's Golden Syrup
800ml freshly squeezed orange juice (about 8 oranges)
200ml freshly squeezed pink grapefruit juice
  (about 1 grapefruit)
juice of a lime
4 shots of Tequila (optional)
4 slices of orange for garnish
4 mint sprigs and ice to serve

In a small pan gently warm the golden syrup together with about a quarter of the orange juice, until it is dissolved. Pour into a large glass jug, add in the other fresh juices and stir until thoroughly mixed. Chill for 1 hour in the fridge.

Put some ice into each glass, pour in the Tequila (if using) and pour the juice mixture over it. Make one cut from the outside to the centre of each orange slice and wedge onto the rim of the glass. Finish with a sprig of mint, serve and then close your eyes and imagine you're in the Caribbean.

A little tip here is to pour the lime juice into an ice tray and freeze it adding it to the drinks giving extra colour, flavour and zing (1 lime makes 2 ice cubes).

THE LYLE'S 125TH ANNIVERSARY CAKE (ORANGE BUTTERCREAM GATEAU)

Just imagine dark chocolate, bitter orange and silky sweet icing wrapped around a beautifully moist and textured celebration cake.

4 medium free-range eggs
75g caster sugar
100g unsalted butter, softened
1 rounded tablespoon Lyle's Golden Syrup
zest of an orange (1 tablespoon)
1 tablespoon orange juice
40g self-raising flour
75g ground almonds
50g fine fresh breadcrumbs

For the decoration
100g candied orange peel
50g dark chocolate
150g unsalted butter
300g icing sugar
1 dessertspoon Cointreau

Preheat the oven to 150C/300F/Gas 2. It is important with this recipe to have all your ingredients ready and a 23cm/9" cake tin lined with baking parchment.

Separate the eggs, with the yolks in one bowl and the whites in another.

Add the caster sugar to the egg yolks and whisk really well until you have a thick, creamy consistency. Lift your whisk from the mixture; draw a figure of 8 with the drizzling cream and if the '8' stays until you have completed the figure it is whisked enough. Now beat in the softened butter, the golden syrup and the orange zest and juice.

Make sure that your whisk is completely clean and free of any grease (otherwise this won't work) and whisk the egg whites until you have really stiff peaks.

Mix the flour, almonds and breadcrumbs together and add them to the egg yolk mixture then fold in the egg whites in a few big airy sweeps. Your mixture will look rather like scrambled eggs.

Pour the mixture into the lined cake tin and bake in the centre of the oven for 1 hour until risen and golden. This is a rich gateâu not a sponge so do not expect it to rise as much. Remove from the oven and leave for 5 minutes before transferring to a wire rack.

While the cake cools prepare the icing and decoration. Chop the butter up into small pieces, place in a mixing bowl and beat until it is smooth and creamy. Gradually add the icing sugar while mixing slowly until it is well combined. Mix in the Cointreau then whisk the icing vigorously until it is smooth and creamy. Chill in the fridge.

Melt the chocolate in a double boiler or in a bowl over a pan of simmering water. Cut the candied peel into little leaf shapes about 5cm long and dip half of each leaf into the melted chocolate. Lay each leaf on some greaseproof paper for the chocolate to set and when all are done chill in the fridge.

When the cake has cooled split it through the middle and spread a third of the icing mixture on the base. Sandwich the cake together again and spread the remainder on the top and round the sides of the cake. You can make a smooth finish with a palette knife otherwise use the back of a spoon or a fork for a more fun effect. Dip a spoon into the remainder of the chocolate and then drizzle very fine strands of chocolate over the butter icing. Finish by adding the chocolate dipped candied orange in a circle on top of the cake.

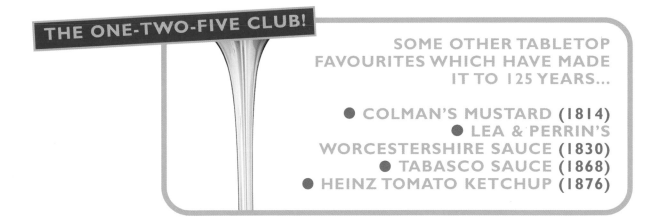

THE ONE-TWO-FIVE CLUB!

SOME OTHER TABLETOP FAVOURITES WHICH HAVE MADE IT TO 125 YEARS...

● COLMAN'S MUSTARD (1814)
● LEA & PERRIN'S WORCESTERSHIRE SAUCE (1830)
● TABASCO SAUCE (1868)
● HEINZ TOMATO KETCHUP (1876)

ONE HUNDRED AND TWENTY-FIVE GOLDEN YEARS
A LITTLE BIT OF HISTORY...

IN THE BEGINNING...

In 1865, Abram Lyle, a successful Scottish businessman, along with four other partners purchased a sugar refinery. When the principal partner died seven years later, Lyle decided to sell up and search for a refinery of his own. In 1881, along with his three sons, he bought two wharves in the east of London to construct a refinery. Melting began two years later, and with it the story of one of the world's oldest and best-loved brands....

over a tonne a week. As demand grew, Golden Syrup dispensers began to appear on the shelves of grocery stores, to pour as much of the golden gloop as customers demanded.

FOUNDING FATHER
ABRAM LYLE

1883

A product from the sugar cane refining process was a sticky syrup which Lyle discovered could be turned into a tasty preserve and used as a natural sweetener for cooking. First referred to as 'Goldie', the amount of syrup produced in those early attempts was modest, but quantities grew and grew and grew. The syrup was poured into wooden casks (a slow job, for sure!) and decanted to a paying customer base made up of employees and sweet-toothed locals. Word inevitably spread and in the space of just a few months, Lyle & Sons were selling

BARREL OF LAUGHS
A CASK OF SYRUP

1885

The ultimate convenience of the tin was never far off, such was the demand for Lyle's fantastic invention. The first tins of Golden Syrup came out of Plaistow just two years after Lyle first thought to extract and also sell his cane sugar as a value-added co-product.

1904

The famous lion-and-bees trademark is registered. Lyle had stout religious beliefs and the imagery and quotation were drawn from the Bible – a passage in the Book of Judges where Samson kills a lion.

1903 GOLDEN RETRIEVERS were first accepted for registration by the The Kennel Club of England, but under the name of Flat Coats – Golden. In 1911, they were recognized as a breed called Retriever with two types – Golden and Yellow. In 1913, the Golden Retriever Club was founded.

1911

The Royal Warrant is awarded to Lyle's Golden Syrup and is promptly displayed on the tin. The warrant acknowledges that the goods advertised are supplied to royal personages or courts, and precious few are handed out. Even fewer are held for as long as Lyle's would go on to hold theirs – 97 years and counting!

1914–1919

During the First World War, metal was in desperately short supply, as all available material was being used for the war effort.

A makeshift cardboard tin was put into production, labelled as follows: 'Owing to the requirements of the Ministry of Munitions with a view to economy in the use of tin plates, we are compelled to adopt this substitute for our usual lever lid tins. There is no change in the quality or weight of the contents'. It represented the first major change to the Lyle's packaging in almost thirty years.

1921

The business started back in 1883 by Abraham Lyle merges with the sugar refinery set up by Henry Tate in 1878 to form Tate & Lyle. The two gentlemen almost certainly never met (despite their refineries being less than two miles apart). It was their descendents who formed the famous partnership and today, 75 years later, Tate & Lyle is the only remaining cane sugar refiner in the UK, and the largest in Europe.

1930 THE GOLDEN BOOT is the award given to the top goal scorer at each football World Cup. Since the competition began in Uruguay in 1930, only once has the award been won by an English player – Gary Lineker, who scored 6 goals at the 1986 Mexico tournament.

1937 AT TWELVE NOON, May 28th, GOLDEN GATE BRIDGE in San Francisco opened to vehicular traffic, an event announced to the world when President Franklin D. Roosevelt pressed a telegraph key in the White House. At the time of opening, it was the longest-spanning suspension bridge in the world.

GOLDEN SYRUP

EASY TO DISPENSE

OLD-STYLE URN

HOME OF GOLDEN SYRUP

THE PLAISTOW WHARF REFINERY

1944 THE GOLDEN GLOBES are American awards for film and television. They started in 1944 as a fundraiser set up by the Hollywood Foreign Press Association. Today, they rank as the third most important awards show in America, behind only the Oscars and the Grammys.

1950

The beginning of the decade which saw the introduction of Lyle's Black Treacle, perfect for treacle tarts, and extending the sweet Lyle's portfolio into a new and exciting era.

1953 THE GOLDEN ARCHES become the symbol of the McDonalds hamburger chain which started in Oakbrook, Illinois, as Dick and Mac McDonald begin franchising their company. In the beginning, one arch stood at either side of what was then simply a walk-up hamburger stand.

1964 "GREETINGS TO YOU, the lucky finder of this GOLDEN TICKET, from Mr Willy Wonka!" These words are reproduced, of course, from Roald Dahl's beguiling novel, *Charlie and the Chocolate Factory*. A factory tour and lifetime supply lay in wait for each finder.

THE FACTORY LINE

WORKERS AT PLAISTOW

1965 THE MAN WITH THE GOLDEN GUN was Francisco Scaramanga – the villain from Ian Fleming's James Bond novel, which was adapted for film 9 years later. Scaramanga is one of the silver screen's most memorable villains by dint of a particularly unusual anatomical feature – a third nipple!

1983

Lyle's Golden Syrup chalks up 100 years – something few other food brands have achieved. The tin has remained largely unchanged during all of that time and production still rolls out from the same refinery that Abram Lyle established over a century ago.

NO FUSS!
THE EASY-POUR BOTTLE

1996

Easy-pour bottles of the syrup are introduced, in original and maple flavours.

2003

A 'Golden Moments' advertising campaign weaves together the uniqueness and versatility of the syrup to remind consumers how delicious it tastes drizzled onto pancakes, porridge and crumble!

2005

Lyle's launch the super ice-cream-friendly Squeezy Syrups! They're available in

2001 The country's most famous couple – the Beckhams – are interviewed on UK chat show, *Parkinson*. Victoria famously reveals her nickname for husband David: 'GOLDENBALLS'.... Cue a thousand and one tongue-in-cheek tabloid headlines, ribbing from team mates and ridicule from the terraces!

2002 THE GOLDEN JUBILEE marked the fiftieth anniversary of Queen Elizabeth II's accession to the throne, with events and celebrations taking place all over the United Kingdom and other Commonwealth realms. Five years later she would become Britain's longest living monarch

MIDAS TOUCH
THE SPECIAL-EDITION GOLDEN TIN

seven different flavours and packed into curvaceous squeezy bottles.

2007

Guinness World Records recognises Lyle's Golden Syrup as having 'the world's oldest branding (packaging) for a brand'.

2008

THE BIG ANNIVERSARY as Lyle's reaches 125 years. Seven special-edition golden tins are designed to commemorate this remarkable milestone.

ACKNOWLEDGEMENTS

When I was first asked to write this book it appeared to be quite a demanding proposition. However, scurrying through my personal recipe book I couldn't believe the variety and volume of recipes I had created over the years using Lyle's Golden Syrup to infuse and develop flavours in all sorts of dishes. Which is why I have to say a big thank you to Marion Veisseire, the Brand Manager at Tate & Lyle for giving me the privilege of writing this cookbook. I can never quite adequately express the extent of my appreciation to my wife, Lynda, who has worked on every recipe with me, sometimes several times, with unending enthusiasm and support – you are a real treasure. Thanks also to Sheila Scott who worked with me to perfect the Anniversary Cake and to Sarah Francis whose technical support and advice has been a crucial part of this book. Then there are thanks to be registered to all our friends who have eaten, commented and supported us for lunches and dinners with Lyle's as the topic of culinary conversation.

This is the fifth cookbook I have had the great pleasure to write with publishers Absolute Press, so my hearty and sincere thanks to Jon Croft for his never-ending support and understanding, and especially to Matt Inwood whose creative genius works wonders on presenting my recipes, and to Meg Avent for her grand efforts as Commissioning Editor.

The publisher would like to thank the following: Marion Veisseire, Ian Clark and Michael Grier and to everyone at Tate & Lyle who gave their help and support.

All food photography and image on pages 72 © Andy Davis.

All other images courtesy of Tate & Lyle PLC.

A
STICKY
END